We are the Undead, or are We? Companion

A Collection of Vampire Articles

Briana Blair

I0415504

We are the Undead, or are We? Companion - A Collection of Vampire Articles

Copyright © 2011, Briana Blair

Cover art by Eric Peacock © 2011

ISBN 978-1-105-31631-9

Contact me:
webmaster@bluedragoncreations.com

Visit my website: bluedragoncreations.com

Find all of my books: bit.ly/thebooks

Table of Contents

Foreword

Do you love vampires? Then you'll love this book. Here you will find topics like: Are you a vampire? What's the difference between real living vampires and the vampires of legend? Psychic feeding for vampires, vampire quotes, vampire cults, online vampire groups and much more. There is a heavy focus on RLVs or Real Living Vampires, but the content here should be both entertaining and educational to any vampire fan.

The following is a collection of articles that I've written over the years concerning various vampire topics. I have enjoyed both the myth and reality of vampires for most of my life, so now I'm sharing that with you. These articles were originally written for Associated Content or my vampire fan site The Vampire's Lair.

I have compiled these articles within this book as a companion to the original *We Are the Undead* book, but it works well as a stand-alone volume. I hope you enjoy the articles and that you learn something new.

Sincerely,

Briana Blair

Please note that my opinions on certain things may have changed between the time I wrote these articles and when I wrote We are the Undead. Also, when writing for my site, I was often evasive or creative in my answers. I did this for the general safety of those reading on the site; I didn't want to encourage impressionable teens into dangerous activity.

Sanguinarians & Real Living Vampires

Medical Explanations for Vampirism

Medical conditions as reason for vampire myth

The following information describes afflictions and diseases that could cause one to be mistaken for a vampire, and scientific "reasoning" as to why one would think themselves to be a vampire.

Anemia:

A blood disease in which the red-cell count of the afflicted is abnormally low. Red blood cells carry oxygen through the body. Symptoms may include: a pale complexion, fatigue, fainting, shortness of breath and digestive disorders. Anemia can be caused by disease, heredity or severe blood loss. Over the years, people suffering these symptoms were often considered to be victims of vampiric attack. The afflicted person's pale complexion and difficulty eating food often caused suspicion that one was becoming a vampire. [More about anemia on WebMD]

Catalepsy:

A nervous system disorder that causes loss of voluntary motion, muscle rigidity and decreased sensitivity to pain and heat. A person suffering from Catalepsy cannot move, but is still able to see and hear. Their breathing, pulse, and bodily functions are slowed to a point that they can be mistaken for dead. Before the 20th century, there were inadequate methods for determining whether or not one was actually dead, and embalming was not yet in practice, which may have caused some sufferers of this condition to be buried while still alive. Upon waking from the cataleptic state, the person may have tried to dig themselves free of the grave, thus explaining the stories of the "undead" rising from the grave. [More about catalepsy on MedTerms]

Porphyria:

A rare hereditary blood disease in which the afflicted is unable to produce heme, a major component of red blood. Symptoms include: photosensitivity, paling of the skin, sores and scars that will not heal, tightening of the skin around the lips and gums (thus making the teeth appear more prominent). Until about fifty years ago, there was no known cure for the disease, which can now be alleviated with injections of heme into the body. The disease would cause one to likely only venture out in darkness to avoid the painful rays of the sun. Also, while garlic is beneficial to a healthy person, it would only exacerbate the symptoms of someone suffering from Porphyria. In times past, it was believed that Porphyria could be cured through blood transfusions, which may have added to the myths of people drinking blood, most likely in an attempt to alleviate their symptoms, rather than as a vampiric act. [More about porphyria on WebMD]

Xeroderma Pigmentosum:

An extremely rare genetic condition in which the afflicted has such severe photosensitivity that exposure to UV rays, particularly from the sun can cause irreparable skin damage and even death. Symptoms include: irritation and blistering after minimal sun exposure, premature aging of skin, eyes, mouth and tongue, blindness, developmental disabilities, high frequency hearing loss and deafness. Sufferers of this condition, like those with Porphyria, would need to be completely sheltered from all sunlight, most likely venturing out only in total darkness. The severe reaction of pain and burning of the skin suffered by victims of XP could, before times of proper diagnosis, have led one to believe that the person was a vampire, since it was commonly thought that vampires were killed by sunlight. [More about XP on XPS.org]

Astral Travel:

There are those who claim to be able to leave their physical body, and move about on the astral plain. If someone was known to be capable of this, it could have led to them being thought of as a witch or vampire. If one were to be visited by the astral body of a person, they may have thought they were being contacted by a vampiric spirit.

Ignorance, the Church, and Lack of Medical Technology:

Before the advent of modern technology, many things would lead one to believe that someone was a vampire. In addition to the previously mentioned symptoms, if one were to be exhumed, and their hair or nails had grown, their skin appeared flushed, their skin was warm, or they had blood at the mouth, they may have been considered to be a vampire. Today we know these to be normal occurrences after death and during decay. It was often considered that a male who had been exhumed and possessed an erection was a vampire. This was actually caused by the expanding gasses in the penis and scrotum that naturally occur after death. This may have led somewhat to the eroticism of vampires, as one would have believed the man to be sexually virile even after death.

Blood on the hands, or a ghastly expression of the face of the exhumed body were also considered signs that they were a vampire. These things were usually caused, in reality, by premature burial due to the inability to properly diagnose a severe health problem. If a body was exhumed and staked (the most popular way of "killing" a vampire, next to beheading), and it groaned or "breathed" it was considered proof that it had been a vampire. We now know that it is not unusual for a body to expel gasses, especially if punctured or impacted, and this could lead to the deceased making "unnatural" sounds. Widespread diseases, such as Bubonic Plague, were often attributed to vampires, and the first person to be afflicted was typically considered to be the vampire. The church had a great deal to do with this. Since there was not effective medical science to explain the plagues, the church looked for supernatural forces to blame.

Turning, Becoming and Awakening

Frequently heard terms in vampire society

These are terms you will hear often in the vampire community. I'll try to define them here to the best of my ability.

Turning

This term is derived from the belief that one can be made into a vampire, or be "turned". Most, if not all, true vampires scoff at this idea. While role-players and movie buffs have clung to the belief that they can become vampires through being bitten, consuming the blood of a vampire or other methods, it is simply not true according to the great majority of practicing vampires. It is the generally held belief that one is born a vampire, and cannot be turned or made by any means. You either have "the hunger" or you don't.

Dressing in black or carelessly feeding on blood does not a vampire make. It is something we have within us that makes us what we are; it cannot be given or taken away. If you ask someone you think to be a vampire to "turn" you, do not expect a pleasant or polite response. You may get lucky and encounter someone with the patience and experience to set you down and tell you the error of your thoughts, but most likely you will be scoffed at, mocked, and/or labeled a "wanna-be".

Becoming and Awakening

These are terms used to define the state of realizing, or coming to terms with the fact that one is a vampire. Of these terms, Awakening seems to be the one most preferred. Awakening can happen at any time, but is generally experienced during or after puberty, but is sometimes not experienced until later in life. Awakening is usually when you first realize that you are different, or that there is something more to life than what you thought you knew.

There are some signs typically associated with awakening, but they do not necessarily indicate vampirism. The symptoms include, but are not limited to, increased sensory sensitivity, such as heightened hearing, smell or sight, including night vision. Many vampires experience sensitivity to and increased awareness of sounds, sights and light. It is quite common for one to notice an aversion or sensitivity to sunlight, a need to shield one's eyes from the sun, and burning easily with minimal sun exposure. One may also notice mood swings, depression, and heightened psychic capabilities, particularly empathy, or the sharing/feeling of other's emotions. Insomnia and increased strength may also be seen. These can be attributed to normal biological changes depending on when they occur, but they could also mean more.

If you're experiencing these things, don't read too much into it until you know all the facts. You are the only one that can decide whether or not you are a vampire. While others may be able to assist you in your decision, in the end it is up to what you feel in your heart and soul as to what you are. Do not allow yourself to be defined by others, you know yourself better than anyone.

As for the term of "becoming", I can't say too much about that. While some use it interchangeably with awakening, some consider "becoming" as the point when you actively pursue your nature and the life of a vampire, whatever that may mean to you. It may mean blood feeding, psi-feeding, taking on a nocturnal habit, or any number of other things. I will leave the definition of this up to you.

Information for Teen Vampires and the "Awakening"

For teens entering the vampire community

It is very important for young people entering the vampire community to know the possible dangers of their decision. There are a lot of scary people out there in the world, looking to prey on the young and the impressionable. If you think you may be a vampire, or are entering into any "vampiric community", there are several things you should keep in mind.

First of all, don't listen to anyone who says that there are specific traits that all vampires have, and if you have them, then you must be a vampire too. While there are many traits associated with vampires, such as pale skin, dark hair, sensitivity to sunlight, intense eye color, heightened senses, and the like, they can also be something as simple as good genetics, or as severe as a true medical condition. While many "real vampires" bear several of the traits you will see splashed across web pages on the 'net, many do not. There is no way to tell just by looking, or going down a list of so-called "traits" of "vampiric signs".

Likewise, your manner of dress is nothing more than a form of personal expression. Dressing all in black doesn't immediately make you Goth or a Vampire. On the flip-side, dressing in "average" style, doesn't mean you're not a vamp, or anything else. If anyone tells you that you have to dress a certain way to be what you are, then they really have no clue what they're talking about. Don't ever feel that you have to dress a certain way, talk a certain way or listen to a certain kind of music to be a vampire, or worry that if you don't you're not one. You are who and what you are; all that other stuff is just a matter of preference.

Read as much as you can on vampirism. Read the myth, the facts, the medical causes, and everything else you can find. The Fact section to the left has a lot of good articles, but read all you can, and don't take any one site's word as gospel. Truth varies from person to person; you will need to find your own truth.

If you are under 18, or even if you are older, I strongly urge you not to go out and tell the world that you think you're a vampire. More likely than not, people will think you're unstable, troubled, or just nuts. Some may even think you're dangerous. Be careful who you tell, and how you tell them. Even family and best friends may not understand. Your best bet is to A: Wait until you are really sure of yourself and what you believe you are, and B: try to bring the topic up gently. Try starting a conversation about a vampire film, and infer that you think such creatures may really exist, but in a different form, or maybe bring up topics of the occult. See how that goes first. If the response is favorable, then try easing into telling them about yourself. Don't expect people to readily accept it. It can take time, and a very open-minded and understanding person. When I came out of the "broom closet" as being Pagan, I was met with a great deal of confusion, misunderstanding and contempt. It has taken years for people to accept my beliefs. Imagine what it is like to "come out of the coffin"! I don't even mention it, though I have had people ask, and that is usually an easy way to get into the topic, even though many of those who ask are very condescending about it.

Even though you may be tempted to tell your best friend or boyfriend/girlfriend, it's not really a good idea, until you are really sure, and only if you believe they will take it well. Especially if you're young, it can be devastating to lose your friends or boy/girlfriend because you outed yourself to them. It's best to keep what you are to yourself. As lonely as it may seem to do so, it is usually the safest option, and will save you from the hassles of needing to explain yourself, and all the heartache that comes with people not understanding what you are. It's especially important to not reveal yourself to your family, particularly if you are under 18 or living at home. Parents get worried, and the last thing you need is to end up battling with your parents over your behavior, or worse, being put in a mental health facility because they think you might hurt yourself or someone else.

If you enter into a forum or chat group, don't go in calling yourself Lestat or Akasha, and ask to be "sired" or "turned". In general, this is considered impossible. Don't be dramatic, and don't be insulting. Try to read up before you start chatting, so you know what you're saying. If you're role-playing, go to forums or chats specifically for role-players. Real vampires can become quite irked at newbies jumping into a conversation with lots of V:TM lingo and sorry attempts at being cool. Just be yourself. "Hey, I'm Jackie and I'm looking for information on whatever topic." You don't need to impress anyone. Just relax, be respectful, and you can learn a lot if you're in the right place.

One of the most important things for younger people who feel they are "awakening" is to be VERY wary of groups, "houses" and things of that nature. Many of these places are more like cults than anything else. If you are asked to become a "childer", someone requests to be your "sire" or people use other terms commonly heard in Vampire: The Masquerade, be careful! It may just be someone role-playing and having fun, but it could just as easily be someone trying to find an impressionable person to manipulate. All those terms and Old English verse can be very enticing to someone who is new to the vampire community.

Also beware of groups that have a "Prince" or "Master". While there may be forms of hierarchy in some groups, if you are expected to obey blindly, or worship anyone, you should go elsewhere, quickly. Research any groups thoroughly before joining or entering. It's best if you know someone who is already a member, and ask them in detail about the practices of the group. You don't want to end up in some cult where you will be hurt or abused. While a group or house may be a wonderful place to be with like-minded people and feel comfortable, I urge you to use caution and common sense before joining any group.

On the same lines, be careful who you give your personal information out to. Especially on the internet, there are a vast number of predators looking for someone that is easily manipulated. Particularly if you are depressed, lonely, or suffering abuse at home, you are a prime target for the sleazy people that surf the 'net looking for victims. Get to know anyone you communicate with before you meet them or give out any personally identifiable information. And always listen to your gut. Does the person sound like they're dangerous? Are they using odd language, like "thou art beautiful" or asking to "sire" or "embrace" you? Are they demanding to meet you with little or no conversation? Are there heavy sexual overtones in their communication? These are all warning signs. Instinct is a God-given gift, don't ignore it. If someone makes you feel odd, or uncomfortable, break off communication, or if you feel you may be in danger, tell a parent, trusted adult, or inform the police.

You should also be careful of what activities you engage in. Blood feeding, like unprotected sex, is a perfect way to contract a disease. Never consume blood from someone that you don't know. Read my Blood Feeding & Safety article for more info on this. Before engaging in any blood activities, you need to know how to protect yourself, and your "donor" or "blood partner". Please keep in mind that you should never engage in cutting, blood play or blood feeding just to be cool. It's not cool. It's very dangerous, and should only be done by mature adults who know the dangers and consequences, as well as the benefits of such activity. You should also never attempt to feed on your own blood. It does you no good at all, and can cause scarring, weakness and mental stress that you really don't need.

Being a vampire is more than just a title you take on to seem cool or creepy among your friends. It is a very serious thing. You don't just wake up one day and decide you're going to be a vampire. It's something that's always in you, though it may take years to discover and understand it. If you are drinking blood or cutting just for the sake of doing it, or for the erotic pleasure of it, you may be a Blood Fetishist, and you might want to look into support groups for it. Being a vampire is typically expressed as having a need, not a desire, for blood or energy. Many vampires would give anything to be "normal". It is not something that one would choose if one had much sense. It doesn't make you cool, or immortal, you aren't guaranteed to get laid more often or be respected by your peers. You are likely to be depressed, isolated, thought of as weird, a freak, a "Goth", and be totally misunderstood. And being a vampire doesn't mean you can't be sick, and having certain symptoms doesn't mean you're a vampire.

Be sure to see a qualified physician if you can't sleep, feel depressed, can't eat, or have any other ailments. Make sure to keep your body as healthy as possible, you don't live forever.

I know all this may sound scary and confusing, and it is. But don't worry. Once you have educated yourself on the topic, and gotten into some good groups, you'll realize you're not alone and will be able to find the information and support you're looking for.

Are You a Teenage Vampire or Just a Normal Teenager?

Symptoms of being a teenage vampire may be the same as natural changes

A lot of teenagers join online vampire communities because they think that they might be vampires. Are they really vamps, or are they just going through normal changes?

Being a teenager can be very confusing. It's a time in your life when everything's changing, and you don't always know what to make of it. A lot of teens, especially in our vampire-saturated age, wonder if they're teenage vampires. They see all the symptoms set out by movies and books, and they start to think that there's more to their changing condition than just hormones.

Nearly every vampire-related book or movie sets out a collection of symptoms that mean you're a vampire, or are likely to become one. Even though most mythology states that vampires are made, not born, a lot of teenagers see these traits in fiction, and in themselves, and they become even more confused than they normally would be. The thing is, a lot of the so-called vampiric traits are also things that occur naturally during human teenage years. Let's discuss some of these traits and what could cause them naturally.

Vampires are almost always beautiful. If you're a teenager and you're suddenly becoming more attractive and appealing to the opposite sex, it could very well be that you're just growing out of the gawky kid stage, and coming into your adult body. Heightened sexual desire and sexual attractiveness fit here as well. Teenagers are full of hormones, and it's natural to become more sexually curious, and to both see others and be seen by others in a more sexual way.

Vampires also tend to have great strength. It is in no way uncommon for a teenager to become stronger and more physically fit as they age. It can even happen so fast, going from clumsy and weak to graceful and strong, that it seems like a near-magical shift. Increased speed goes right along with this, following in the footsteps of naturally improving physical abilities. Heightened senses are an extremely common trait of Hollywood vampires. This is also something that can happen naturally. As you grow up your senses may improve, or you may just become more aware of them. Improvements in your senses can happen to anyone at any time though, it's especially common in menstruating or pregnant women.

Some of the more odd traits would be changing eye color, growing fangs, and developing psychic powers. While uncommon, some people's eye color can change with age, or even with mood. Growing fangs after you've already lost baby teeth is rare, but possible. It isn't uncommon at all however, for people to grow hyper-extended canines after shedding their baby teeth. My eyes change color based on mood and I have naturally hyper-extended canines, so both can even happen in one person. As for psychic abilities like empathy, clairvoyance and others, I have always believed that these can occur in anyone, and I have never found any correlation between increased psychic abilities and real vampirism.

Long story short, most of the traits that you might have seen or read about really won't tell you if you're a real teenage vampire or not. You're most certainly not a vampire of myth and legend, but whether or not you're a Real Living Vampire is something that is harder to discover. Vampirism is typically defined by a need (not just a desire) to feed off other beings in the form of blood or pranic energy. If this is not something you feel, all of your other symptoms could well be natural parts of growing up.

If you're still not sure whether or not you may be a teenage vampire, I would suggest seeking out a reliable online vampire community, joining their forums, and asking around. Do some research, and make sure you see your family doctor to rule out any health issues. (Although I wouldn't suggest telling your family physician that you think you might be a vampire.) If you know you're physically healthy, and you know the difference between Real Living Vampires and the vampires of lore and fiction, talking to others in a similar situation is a good next step. People who have already gone through what you're going through will be able to help you find the answers you need.

Is My Friend Really a Vampire?

Attempting to answer a difficult question

This is one of those questions that some people are going to hate me for answering, because they're not going to like what I have to say. Simply put, more likely than not, if you know someone who goes around saying that they're some 100 plus year old vampire with all kinds of abilities that they refuse to show you, they're most likely not.

Don't get me wrong; I believe that vampires, albeit not like the ones in the movies, could really exist. And depending on how one defines the term "vampire", it could actually be true, but in most cases, it's not. Many people with boring, unfulfilling lives will get caught up in a fantasy world, and will lose track of reality, and start to believe that their own fiction is truth. These are people who need someone gentle and understanding to give them a tactful reality check, and encourage them to seek counseling.

If vampires are indeed real, it's not likely in our current society that they'd go around bragging about it. Think about it, it's still not even safe to be gay or Pagan in many parts of the world, how safe do you think it would be to be a vampire or werewolf or some such? You'd be hunted, experimented upon, ostracized… it would be a dangerous and horrible life. Now, there is the small chance that if vampires propagate by "turning", as most legends suggest, and someone was turned too young, they might have enough of a rebellious streak to go out and blab to the world, trying to bring their kind out of the shadows. However, even this wouldn't account for the vast numbers of people that even I, personally, have seen claim themselves to be centuries old beings. Most of these people are looking for attention, trying to be cool, and are lost in a fantasy world that is more interesting and exciting than their real lives.

Now, earlier I mentioned that there are some uses of the term "vampire" that could be accurate. Examples would be someone like a sanguinarian, as people that feed on blood might classify themselves as vampires. Also, people who have learned to feed on the energies of other people sometimes call themselves "psi-vamps", or "psychic vampires". Vampire can also be used in a negative connotation, referring to someone who drains others, such as a person who's constantly displaying traits of self-loathing and self-pity, may be considered a "social vampire" because they do, in a sense, drain the life out of a social group.

If you know someone who is claiming to be a vampire, find out what they mean by it. If it is something they can explain, like my previous examples, then you may let it slide. If they're claiming to be older than dirt with mystical powers and whatnot, you may want to have a talk with them. If it seems to be adversely affecting his or her social life, you might want to tell someone else, such as a parent or counselor, especially if it's a young person. Also, keep your eyes open for dangerous behavior like cutting themselves or others, violent and antisocial behavior, and talk of criminal activity. These can be signs of a serious mental problem, and you should definitely talk to someone that can help them.

In closing, the likelihood that you know a real vampire is slim, but not impossible. Theoretically it is possible that a real vampire might find you worthy of the trust involved in revealing their true identity. However, you are likely dealing with someone who has spent a bit too long in their own fantasy world. Playing a vampire now and again for fun is fine, pretending, even for an adult, can often be a healthy escape for the doldrums of daily life. But if it becomes a WAY of life, it could be a real problem.

What Kind of Vampire Am I?

Are you a Sang, Psi or some other type of vampire?

There are a few different recognized types of vampire in Real Vampire society. This article will help you know which type you are, or if you're a vampire at all.

Let me start off by saying that this article is about Real Living Vampires, not mythical, Hollywood or role-playing vampires. This is a guide for real people, in the real world. Deciding whether you're a vampire or not, and if so, what kind, is a serious thing, and should not be taken lightly.

There are a few major types of real vampire: Sanguinarian, Psychic, Hybrid and Lifestyle vamp. Each type has its own characteristics, and most people identify with a single type, although the types can intermingle in some ways. If you consider yourself to be a vampire, it's a good idea to know which kind you are. Knowing what type you are will help you greatly in finding information and connecting with other people in vampire society.

Lifestyle Vampire

Lifestyle vampires are not necessarily "real" vampires, as they do not need to feed on energy. Lifestyle Vampire refers to people who dress and act in a manner that they believe represents the persona of a true vampire. They will often wear Victorian or Gothic style clothing, speak in period language, and act as if they have a high social standing. Some people consider Lifestyle Vampires to be posers, while others accept them as part of the subculture. Sangs, Psys and Hybrids can also be Lifestyle Vampires, combining their real need for feeding with their clothing and lifestyle choices.

Sanguinarian Vampire

A Sanguinarian vampire is someone who has a need to feed on blood. Sanguinarians are different from blood fetishists because the acquisition of blood is considered a necessity, not a matter of erotic pleasure. Not to say that Sanguinarians never experience erotic pleasure from feeding, but it is not their primary interest.

At one time a Sanguinarian would have only fed on human blood, and some still consider this the only way to satisfy their needs and survive. Some Sangs will feed on animal blood, although most find it unclean and unsatisfying. As time has gone by, many Sanguinarians have drifted away from blood feeding and begun learning to Psy feed, due to the large number of transmittable diseases that currently exist. Real Vampires do not have any illusions of being immortal or invulnerable, they know all too well of the dangers of feeding on blood, but it is a need they must satisfy in some form.

Psychic Vampire

Psychic Vampires feed on energy rather than blood. Some people are natural Psy Vamps, while others have learned to be such. Psychic Vampires typically prefer to draw energy from other people, but can draw from any living thing, and with practice, from nature itself. Due to the spread of diseases, many Sanguinarians are learning to feed on energy instead of blood for the safety of themselves and the community at large.

Hybrid Vampire

Hybrid Vampires are those who feed on both blood and energy. Some people have always been Hybrid, while others have come to it out of a need to find blood alternatives.

Conclusion

When someone is first "awakening" or realizing that they are a vampire, they may wonder where they fit in. Many automatically assume that feeding on blood is the only option. It's important for an awakening vampire to determine how they will feed, and where they fit in vampire society. It can be a hard road if you don't know what you are and can't ask for help.

Obviously, there's more to each of these types and their practices than I have gone into here. I will be writing an extensive series of articles on Real Vampires, so you may want to check back for more information.

Blood Feeding & Safety

Tips for blood-feeding sanguinarians

Sanguinarians or "sangs" are vampires that feed on blood. Although the need or desire for blood energy is common among what most consider "real" vampires, it can be very dangerous. Please use utmost caution when blood feeding.

Keep in mind these are simply my suggestions and views, and may or may not reflect those of the vampire community in general.

Safety

Contrary to some people's belief, neither modern vampires in general, nor sanguinarians in particular, are immortal or immune to disease. We can all die. For this reason, it is absolutely imperative that you know for a fact that both you and your donor are free of blood-born diseases. HIV, AIDS and STDs are a real threat. You must get yourself and your donor tested prior to any exchange of bodily fluids. Don't go on the assumption that your donor "looks" like a clean person, or take their word that they are disease free. As a matter of safety, courtesy and trust, both parties should be fully tested.

It is also unwise to have multiple donors, unless you again make sure that each one is tested. And be tested regularly!! You can never be too safe, and it is always possible that through donation, sexual contact or drug abuse, that a donor or feeder may become infected after initial testing. (Personally, I would strongly suggest steering clear of persons with "tracks" or other signs of drug abuse, as not only do they have a greater risk of becoming infected with disease, they may also not be in their right mind or fit to consent to donating.)

Be sure you are open and honest with your donor. Discuss testing, your method of feeding, and if your comfortable enough, you may even want to address any issues of promiscuity that could endanger you or your donor. Be sure your donor understands the potential risks, the benefits, and all other issues involved. Discuss how they would like to donate, how much you will derive from the feeding, etc.

Another misconception (to my knowledge anyway) is that sanguinarians feed from the donor by biting the neck or other body parts. From all I know, this is quite untrue. Biting is generally quite painful, can cause severe scarring, and is also a very dirty method of feeding. The human mouth has numerous germs and bacteria that can cause infection in the donor. Typically, blood feeding is done by making a small incision on the body of the donor, just deep enough to draw blood, and the blood is collected in a glass or other receptacle and consumed immediately. Preferences vary as to whether the sang or the donor makes the incision. Discuss this with your donor to see what they are more comfortable with.

If you absolutely insist on putting your mouth on the wound to feed directly, I suggest a thorough brushing of your teeth beforehand, and a lengthy rinse and gargle with antiseptic mouthwash, but infection of the donor is still a strong possibility. You also need to make sure that your tools and the area of the donor to be cut are very clean. If you use a razor or scalpel, soak it for at least 5 minutes in rubbing alcohol, then wash it in hot water and dry it. Then hold it over a flame on each side for about 3 seconds, wipe it with alcohol again, and dry it one last time. Try to keep your tools sealed in a clean, dry place when not in use, and clean them before and after each use.

Always use a very sharp instrument, to minimize pain and damage to the donor. Also, swab the donor area with rubbing alcohol or other antiseptic prior to making the incision. Be sure not to cut your donor too deep! After you have acquired the blood you need, immediately offer your donor a sterile pad or band-aid and some type of antiseptic like Neosporin or Bacitracin. Syringes are also an option for some, but this is to be done with extreme caution as well. If you do not have the proper knowledge, you can seriously injure your donor, and needles must be disposed of immediately after use, and cannot be used again. (Don't get the wrong idea here, I have never heard of a sanguinarian injecting themselves with the donor blood, but I have heard of a rare few who use this as a method of extraction, then the blood is emptied into some sort of drinking vessel.)

Some people seem to think that sanguinarians need massive amounts of blood from their donors. This is almost always untrue. Only a small amount of blood is needed at one time to provide the necessary energy. If you are a donor and your sang even indicates the desire to make a large cut, a deep cut, or go anywhere near a major vein, you may want to leave... Quickly! Nearly all serious sanguinarians care very much for the comfort and safety of their donors, and would never suggest such things. The feeding process is a bonding of sorts with the sang and the donor, and they will want you to be as safe and comfortable as possible. Also, Sanguinarians are still biologically human, and the human stomach is not designed to digest blood. Too much will make one quite ill.

It is also uncommon for a sanguinarian to feed on animal blood. Most consider animal blood a dirty substance, and also, animals are not able to consent to being fed upon. I have heard some sangs say that animal blood is a viable substitute for human blood though. Those who have said such, indicate that cow blood is best, as it carries fewer diseases than pig or chicken blood. Apparently it also tastes better. Some also consume raw/rare meat when blood is not available. I personally have no experience in this field, but with all the diseases that animals carry, I would be wary of this choice.

There is also the concept of "dead blood". This refers to the notion that it is not the blood itself that sustains a vampire, but the energy contained within it. If the blood is not consumed immediately, those vital energies die, and the blood is useless. I have heard varying opinions on this. Some believe the blood must be consumed immediately, while others claim the blood is just as effective if it has been properly stored and consumed at a later time. I believe fresh blood is more useful to the person feeding, but this is a debate I will not enter into at this point.

I have also heard of people consuming their own blood. This does no good if you are truly a sanguinarian. All you will succeed in doing is depleting your own energy. Feeding must be done from a source other than oneself in order to be effective.

Overview

In closing, just remember to always be safe. Don't hurt your donor, or endanger yourself. Blood Feeding is a very dangerous practice, and should not be entered into lightly. Consuming blood will not make you super-human, it will not make you immortal, and it could potentially kill you. Weigh the benefits and risks carefully before feeding for the first time, and if possible, consult with more experienced sanguinarians to gain as much information as possible.

Eventually I will add an article to this series about psychic and elemental feeding, which in this day and age are considered much safer ways of deriving energy. Though some may consider this an unworthy method for "true" vampires, I think it will warrant further discussion in the future.

Long Distance Psychic and Energy Feeding for Vampires

How can a psychic vampire feed without a local donor?

For some psy-vamps (psychic vampires), feeding can be a challenge because they are unable to find a local energy donor. Fear not though, long-distance feeding might be an option for energy vampires.

How to feed without a local donor is a problem that I have been facing for some time. It can take a real toll on your body and mind if you don't get the energy you need, but what do you do when you have no one nearby who's willing to be a donor? Some vamps will feed off unsuspecting people, but I have issues with that. Most psychic vampires feel that it is wrong to feed off someone without their knowledge and consent. Some energy vamps feel that feeding off crowds is acceptable, so long as you don't feed primarily from any one person. I've had personal issues with feeding off anyone without consent. Desperate for an answer, I started poking around my online RLV (Real Living Vampire) community boards, and drifted into chat where I found an answer.

I'd hear of long distance psychic feeding, and even tried it a time or two. The person I wanted to feed from was unaware though, and it seemed to make it impossible, probably because of my consent issues. Luckily, you can meet people online who are willing to be long-distance energy donors for psy-vamps. I met one of them recently, and I'm very glad I did.

We started off in the forum's chat area and moved over to a private Yahoo chat. We talked a bit, then she opened herself to psychic feeding, and I was able to form a connection to her. It was wonderful! I never thought it would be possible to connect to someone on the other side of the country, but it happened just as easily as feeding from someone in the same room. Satiated, I realized I'd found my solution.

I wish I'd found someone like this years ago. For those psychic vampires out there who aren't in a vampire-friendly area, I would highly recommend finding a donor online. If you go to a reputable group, you can probably find someone who will fit your needs. While I was feeding, I felt something else very interesting, and I think it's worth mentioning.

For this particular energy feeding session, we were both sitting at our computers. I imagined drawing her energy through her computer, over the internet, and into me. I quickly realized that there was much more energy flowing to me than just my donor's. So what was the other energy? I have a theory: When people are sitting at their computers, they are putting a certain amount of energy into them as they do whatever they're doing. By drawing through the internet, I think I was also grabbing some of that energy.

Now, I thought about the fact that I was taking that energy without those people's knowledge or consent. However, I don't think it is unethical in this case. Whenever you do anything, you are willingly putting energy into that act. You know that you're expending energy, and you're getting your desired result. Once the energy is out there, you usually don't give any thought to what happens to it. With this being the case, the energy has already been freely given, and thus there is no ethical issue in using some of it.

Overall, I'm very glad that I decided to go looking into long-distance psychic feeding, and I'm thrilled that I found an energy donor, as well as a way to draw even more energy. I intend to see if I can feed exclusively on energy expended into the internet. If this is possible, it may be a discovery worth sharing with the RLV community to aid other psychic vampires.

Vampire Cult Warning Signs

Ways to spot and avoid Vampire cults

Cults are something to be avoided at all costs. Unfortunately, cults often use appealing subcultures as a ruse to lure people into their grasp. If you're thinking about joining a vampire group, you need to know what to look for to ensure it's not dangerous.

Real Living Vampires sometimes have groups in which they gather, and they can be a good way for people to connect and socialize in a safe environment. However, cults will often use the allure of vampires to draw people into their grasp and do unmentionable things to impressionable people. Before joining a vampire group, check for the warning signs that they might actually be a cult.

Sexual Activity

If sexual activity of any kind is an expected or required part of membership into the group, run. You should never enter into any group that expects you to perform any type of sexual act. Cults frequently require sexual submission as proof of faith and obedience to the group or its leader. Some cults will use terms like "concubine", "courtesan" or "paramour" as a way of confusing or convincing people into engaging in sexual activity.

Beratement and Submission

If the people in the group berate, belittle or insult you as part of "initiation" or common activity, this can be another warning sign. Making people feel that they are worthless and useless is often a way of opening them up to brainwashing and abuse. Also, no legitimate group will expect you to be submissive to other members. Cults often require submissiveness, but legitimate groups will treat all members with respect no matter their standing.

Forced Acts

No legitimate group will expect you to do anything against your will. Real Vampires believe that all should come to the path of their own free will, and find their own way with the support of the community. If you encounter a group that even attempts to force you to do anything against your will, it is likely not a safe group to be involved with. If you ever get the feeling that you don't want to do something, and someone tries to force or convince you to despite your apprehensions, I would suggest leaving immediately.

Secrecy and Lies

Real vampires like to keep their lives private, and typically don't like word of their groups being spread to the general populous. However, they will not require absolute secrecy or lying. Cults frequently require total secrecy, insisting that there is no one you can trust, and will encourage you to lie about your whereabouts and involvement. There's a big difference between discretion and forced secrecy.

Brainwashing

Brainwashing is often the hardest trait to spot in cults. Their leaders are often highly charismatic and their members blindly faithful. However, if anyone in a group tries to convince you of things that give you a bad feeling, or seem utterly untrue, they may be trying to brainwash you. Unfortunately, truth can be unsettling and hard to accept, so lies and truth can sometimes have the same effect. Cults will go to extremes to convince you that their way is the only way, and all else is lies. Real vampires are glad to educate those truly searching for answers, but will never tell you that their way is the only way, or that any one person's word is gospel.

Overview

Before joining any group, whether it is for vampires, a religion, or any other subculture, it's a good idea to look into them as much as possible. Cults come in many types, and are sometimes simply referred to as "extremist groups" or "clans". No matter what they're called or what they use to draw people in, they're dangerous. If something feels off about the group, your gut may well be right. Listen to your instincts.

While vampire and Satanic cults are the ones we hear of most, be aware that a cult can use anything to lure people. There have been more than a few cults based around mainstream religion, sexual liberation and other themes. Be careful of who you involve yourself with. There are some wonderful legitimate groups out there, and they won't be hard to find if you do your research.

Online Real Vampire Community Treats Newcomers with Disrespect

Rude treatment and lack of help may effect vampire newbies

Online Real Vampire communities are supposed to be a place for those seeking knowledge to come for information, understanding and a sense of family. When long-time members treat newcomers with disrespect, can it have a negative effect?

I have been a part of the online real vampire community in one form or another since 1996. I was there back in the days of email groups and Mirc chats up through the current forums and live chats. Granted, life has taken me away from the community from time to time. It's that time away that has brought this serious issue back into my mind.

I joined an online real vampire forum group many years back (which shall remain nameless to protect the innocent), and for quite some time I was very active. I was well known and fairly respected. Due to conflicts with another member who I also knew in real life and other personal issues, I left the community and was gone for the better part of two years. When I decided it was time to come back to my "family" I found that I had been purged for inactivity. Not really a big deal, it's something that can happen on any forum. So I signed up again using my old name that everyone knew, and jumped back in.

At first things seemed to be going well. A few of the old-timers welcomed me back, and people I'd never met before did the same. I started talking, reading and posting, and all seemed fine until I went into the live chat. The first time in chat was good, I reconnected with some people and had a good time. The second time in chat caused me to take a week off to cool down so I didn't lash into anyone.

I was having a conversation with a user I knew, and I was asking if they could help me find some information I was after. They were about to point me in the right direction when someone piped in with a comment of "d*mn newbies, expect everything handed to them on a silver platter." Other disparaging newcomer remarks were also made, as if I weren't right there reading them. I never got the information I asked for, and I ended up off in a private chat with someone so I wouldn't lay into that rude user.

Now, granted, part of my anger lies in the fact that I am in no way a noob to the real vampire community, or even that forum. Several people have pointed out that I'm returning after a purge. So I was insulted to receive the disrespect even though my long standing in the community had been vouched for. What made me more angry however, was the fact that old-timers would treat someone they perceived to be new in the vampire community with such disrespect.

If I were a new member, treating me that way could have caused me to have any number of reactions. Some newcomers would have ignored the rude party and continued on, some would have left the community and gone elsewhere for information, some may have left and never found what they needed to know, and for others it may have been the last straw and caused them to commit suicide. I know that sounds extreme, but it could very well happen, and probably has.

Someone, especially a younger person, coming into a real vampire community looking for information and guidance is already in fragile state. They are wondering who and what they are, feeling lonely and misunderstood, and searching for people who will understand them. Being treated disrespectfully and with such disregard could easily drive someone over the edge. If people in a vampire subculture that is supposed to embrace the strange outcasts can't even understand or respect them, who ever could?

I've never really understood this mentality of long-time members treating newcomers like dirt. Now, not all of the old-timers do this, some are gentle and kind and treat people properly. But the bad apples tend to make a big impression. Perhaps they don't think of their actions as out of line, but they certainly are, and they do not paint a good picture of the real vampire community as a whole. I suggest that these people think of their behavior as it would relate in real life.

For one thing, asking a more established member of the community for help is showing respect, and admitting that you are bowing to their greater knowledge. Newcomers are like students, and the older members like teachers. When a student asks their teacher a question, it is appropriate to either give the answer or point them in the right direction, not to insult them for not having gone out and found the answer for themselves already.

You can also think of it this way: If you adopted a child and they asked where the cereal was kept, would you tell them where it was, and acquaint them with other items in their new home, or would you tell them to buzz of and find it for themselves? If a new neighbor came to your door and asked where the post office or a good restaurant was located, would you share your knowledge of the area, or tell them to get lost and use Google or the phone book? Most of us would never be this rude and make such a bad impression on new people.

It's also similar to going to a shopping center or library. Do you spend countless hours wandering the aisles trying to find what you need, or do you lean on the expertise of the staff and ask them to direct you to the right place? The mentality of telling new community members to stop asking questions and find their own answers, especially in a forum with more information than you could wade through in a year, is insane and insensitive. I have always been more than happy to point a newcomer in the right direction. I will even answer a question that's been asked many times before. It's just the right thing to do.

I intend to ask the members of this real vampire community to read this article. Hopefully it will open their eyes to the way they treat new members, and cause them to act in a more friendly and helpful manner. The older and presumably wiser members of the community should lead by example and always show respect and understanding in the community, to all members both old and new. You are teachers and leaders, perhaps you should act as such.

Fiction, Myth & Pop Culture

If Vampires Are Real, What Else is Too?

Could there be many types of supernatural creature?

If you found out that vampires were real, wouldn't you start to wonder what other supernatural creatures are real too?

As a big fan of True Blood, I've actually given some thought to what would happen if vampires "came out of the coffin" and made their existence known to the world. If you set all of the directly vampire-related issues aside, there is something else that might arise out of the discovery that vampires are real. People would likely start to wonder what else that goes bump in the night might be real too.

If there are vampires out there, would that mean that there are werewolves too? In a great deal of fiction, both movies and books, vampires and werewolves exist in the same world, and have been enemies at war for centuries. What if werewolves did exist? If vampires came out would the weres come out too? Would their hate for each other (if that part's true) spill out into the human world?

If there were vampires and were-creatures, could there also be the possibility of shapeshifters? It'd probably be pretty easy for a shifter to blend into normal society, and we'd never know it. If they did exist. How would it affect the world? How would your life change if you knew that the fly on your wall, the bird on your window ledge or the stray dog in your yard might actually be a person? People might become extremely paranoid if that were true and the public knew about it.

People could easily go insane trying to think about all the things that might exist if we had proof that supernatural beings of any kind existed. What about succubi, incubi, sirens, or physically manifested deities? What about trolls, faeries, pixies and other beings? The list could go on forever. And one has to keep in mind the possibility that vampires, weres and any of these other creatures may not be what film and literature have lead us to believe they are. They might be something completely unexpected, and may have been among us since the beginning of time.

Of course, there's also the possibility that any number of supernatural creatures might be aliens. That would really blow people's minds. Imagine if you found out that not only are these beings real, but that they came from other planets? There might be a mass global panic if we found out there were extraterrestrial beings living alongside us.

I have a feeling that even if one or more types of supernatural being really exist, they probably won't ever expose themselves to the public. Humans pretty much hate everything they don't understand, and it's likely that many people would try to kill these "abominations". It would be safer for them to stay hidden, and only reveal their identities to individuals that they trust. The world at large may never be ready to know if things which are not human are living here on Earth with us.

Do Vampires Really Exist?

Do vampires exist, and would we know if they did?

The following are answers to some often asked questions about vampires, both real and mythical.

Do vampires really exist?

Well, that depends on what we're talking about. There are definitely a large number of humans with vampiric traits, vampiric lifestyles and the like. Now if you're referring to the type of vampires we see in movies and read about in books, that's a whole other question entirely. I've never met one myself (at least not that I'm aware of) but I don't put anything outside the realm of possibility.

What are real vampires like?

Having never met and interviewed one, I can't say for certain, but I have my theories on what a real vampire would be like. Everyone has their own ideas. Every myth and legend, every book and movie has an effect on what people think a real vampire would be like. Personally, I think Hollywood's depiction is pretty far off, but that's just my opinion.

If vampires truly exist, I don't think they're demons or monsters. I think they'd probably just be some genetic variation, something that just took a different evolutionary road than the rest of us. I figure vampirism would either be a genetic trait passed down through the generations, or perhaps a communicable disorder of sorts. Most legends seem to have it that vampires are incapable of standard forms of reproduction, but I doubt that would be true. A creature without reproductive ability wouldn't make sense, and I doubt the likelihood of it being an affliction that causes sterility.

I don't believe that vampires would be immortal either. Of course, if you pay attention, the fictionalized vampires aren't really immortal either; they're just amazingly damage resistant. I think it's possible that vampires might age at a reduced rate, thereby giving them a seriously extended lifespan, but I don't really believe in immortality. I'd wager that their systems would fight the signs of aging well, and it would appear that they never get any older, but if one lived long enough to keep track, they'd see the signs eventually.

I don't really think they'd be limited to living in the darkness as many believe. I think they might prefer it, but most likely they could go out in the daytime like anyone, it just might not be as comfortable. I can see the skin and eyes having increased sensitivity to light and UV rays, but I don't think spontaneous combustion would be a worry for them.

I also hold no belief in the idea that real vampires would be shape shifters, have incredible super-human powers, or anything of the like. If anything, I think they'd just be more tapped into the already existing potential of the human mind and body. We are amazingly complex creatures, and few of us ever even reach half of our potential abilities. I think vampires most likely would have evolved in such a way that they would naturally use more of their brain and physical abilities than average people.

Would we know if vampires actually existed?

Probably not. I think if they really exist, they probably blend in so well that we would never know. I wouldn't even be surprised if they wouldn't all know what they are. I don't know if we will ever know for sure if they do, or ever have, existed. If they are real, they probably wouldn't broadcast it on the nightly news. I mean, if you're a higher form of life than the rest of the population, you probably want to keep it that way. If people knew vampires existed, and there was a way to transfer it, millions of people would want to be that way. The rest of the people would probably want to kill the new-found abomination. Either way, it wouldn't be worth it to blab around about it.

Would it be worth it to become a vampire, if it was possible?

Heh, now there's a big question. I guess it depends on the person, and weighing the pros and cons for their particular situation. I'm one of those people that would probably jump on the opportunity if vampires were like I think they are. A lot of others would think the trade-offs weren't worth the risk. Until we find out if they're real, and if they are, what they're really like, I don't think anyone could say for sure whether or not they'd want to be one.

Why are people so obsessed with the idea of vampires?

Think about it... Youth, beauty, sensuality, immortality, power... it's all pretty tempting. Even if it was just a matter of slowed aging, resistance to disease and increased mental acuity, it still sounds like a pretty good deal. Of course, over they years, vampires have become more romanticized and sensualized than they ever were before. No longer are they the hideous demons of lore. Everybody wants to be something better than they are, and the idea of being a vampire, for many, equates to the possibility of being everything that they can never be as plain old boring humans.

In conclusion...

We may never know the truth about the existence of vampires. We know about humans living as such, and the growing popularity of the fascination with vampires. Maybe one day we'll know. Maybe they'll be all the wonderful things we want them to be, maybe they'll be all the horrid things we fear they'd be. If I ever find out, I'll be sure to let you know. *wink*

My Vampire Theory, If They're Real

What I think vampires, if they exist, really are and are not

I've given it a lot of thought over the years, and I have some theories and beliefs about what vampires really are and are not, if they actually exist.

I suppose the first thing I should say is that yes, I do believe that vampires may be walking among us. I know for a fact that there are RLVs (Real Living Vampires) but I also believe that there may be a more supernatural being as well. However, I doubt very highly that they bear much resemblance to the vampires of myth and movies.

First off, I have never subscribed to the idea of vampires being some undead, walking corpse monster. I think the living dead idea came from ages ago, before the invention of proper medical science, when people were often buried alive, and people misidentified the signs of natural decay as signs of ongoing life. It is my belief that vampires are alive, like anything else that walks this Earth. Whether they are born or made is still a grey area for me.

I'm not quite sure where I stand on the idea of vampires being non-human or demons. I believe supernatural and entirely non-human creatures could exist, but I'm not sure about the idea of some escaped hell-spawn in a human visage. I do feel that if vampires exist, they are either a similar creature to humans, but not exactly Homo Sapiens, or they are an evolutionary offshoot that evolved faster and better than humans.

I do believe in the possibility that vampires would possess "super-human" abilities, but not to the extent depicted in so many works of fiction. I doubt very highly that they could fly, run too fast to see, levitate or transform into bats. I don't think they'd have the strength to uproot trees with a single hand. I do believe it's entirely possible for them to be stronger, faster, smarter and more adept than average humans. Some "normal" people have seemingly impossible strength, intelligence or other abilities, so there's no reason to think vampires might not actually be the best or the next level of human ability.

As for powers of the mind such as "glamoring", telepathy, empathy and other abilities, I have no doubt they could possess these. I know that there are already people in the world that possess these abilities. Vampires could easily have perfected these skills, or be born with more proclivity towards them and therefore be naturally adept. If vampires are an advanced species, they could easily have minds more capable of manipulation and higher awareness.

As far as all of the things vampires fear, like garlic, crosses, silver, holy water etc., I think all of that is nonsense. In all my research I have found no real basis for any of these claims. Most of the beliefs tend to stem from a religious background; things the Church believed would ward off evil and demons. Other items are based from local myths and folklore. I assume that a stake through the heart, beheading and being lit on fire would kill anything, so at least those few make sense.

As for the idea of all vampires being sterile and only able to add to their numbers by infecting humans, that doesn't make much sense either. It would make much more sense for vampires to be able to reproduce normally, if vampirism is a state in which you are born. I've considered the possibility that vampirism is a disease of sorts, in which case transmission by blood would be more logical.

Of course, most people wonder why, if vampires exist, we have no concrete proof. If vampires in a super-human advanced sense actually exist, do you think they would want the world to know? Humans have a wonderful way of exploiting or destroying anything they don't understand. Vampires would likely do their best to blend with society and go utterly unnoticed. If they were to come out into the open, a-la True Blood, the death toll would probably be astronomical.

If vampires and all their abilities became public knowledge, the medical world would want to experiment on them, droves of people would flock to be "turned" and masses of religious extremists and bigots would set out on a global witch hunt to kill them. It is more likely that if they exist, they keep their numbers low, and keep their existence virtually unknown. Perhaps one day humans will be enlightened enough to accept the existence of higher beings, but that time certainly has not come yet.

Real Vampires Vs. Hollywood Vampires Part 1

How are they similar, how are they different?

The list below will show some of the similarities and differences between Real Living Vampires (RLVs), Hollywood & Folklore Vampires (H&F), and Role Players (RPGers).

Are they Immortal?

- **RLVs:** No. They can be killed and die like anyone else. They are, after all, human.

- **H&F:** In a sense. They can live for centuries, but are not truly immortal, because there are methods by which they can be destroyed.

- **RPGers:** No. They can be killed and die like anyone else. They are, after all, human.

Some RPGers may claim to be immortal, but they really aren't.

Can they be killed by sunlight?

- ⋏ **RLVs:** No, unless they have Xeroderma Pigmentosum, a serious disorder whereby severe burning and even death can result from even short exposure to the sun.

- ⋏ **H&F:** It depends on the story. Usually vampires can be killed by sunlight, but in more modern tales, the sun us simply uncomfortable, but not deadly.

- ⋏ **RPGers:** No, unless they have Xeroderma Pigmentosum, a serious disorder whereby severe burning and even death can result from even short exposure to the sun. Some RPGers may pretend to have a major aversion to the sun, but it's usually just part of the role.

Can they be killed by stakes, beheading or fire?

⋏ **RLVs:** Yes. These methods would kill pretty much anything, living or undead.

⋏ **H&F:** Yes. These methods would kill pretty much anything, living or undead.

⋏ **RPGers:** Yes. These methods would kill pretty much anything, living or undead.

Are they Goth?

⋏ **RLVs:** Some, but not all. It's a matter of personal preference.

⋏ **H&F:** Some, but not all. It's a matter of personal preference and the time in which the story is set.

⋏ **RPGers:** Some, but not all. It's a matter of personal preference.

Do they dress in Old English or Victorian clothes?

- ⅄ **RLVs:** Not usually, unless it's a special occasion or costume party.

- ⅄ **H&F:** Some, but not all. It's a matter of personal preference and the time in which the story is set.

- ⅄ **RPGers:** Some, but not all. It's a matter of personal preference.

Do they have "superhuman" powers?

- ⅄ **RLVs:** No. While they may have heightened senses or what seems to be abnormal strength, it's usually just a matter of training or good genetics.

- ⅄ **H&F:** Yes. Nearly all H&F vampires are stronger, faster and smarter than humans.

- ⅄ **RPGers:** No. While they may have heightened senses or what seems to be abnormal strength, it's usually just a matter of training or good genetics. Some RPGers may claim to have superhuman powers, but they don't.

Real Vampires Vs. Hollywood Vampires Part 2

How are they similar, how are they different?

The list below will show some of the similarities and differences between Real Living Vampires (RLVs), Hollywood & Folklore Vampires (H&F), and Role Players (RPGers).

Can they read minds, or take energy?

- **RLVs:** Possibly. Some people may truly have psychic abilities, be talented empaths, or have the ability to focus energy.

- **H&F:** Usually. Vampires are often depicted as having power over the minds of "lesser beings". Some are depicted as being able to weaken or control their victims purely by will.

- **RPGers:** Possibly. Some people may truly have psychic abilities, be talented empaths, or have the ability to focus energy. RPGers sometimes make more of their abilities than what is real.

Do they drink blood?

- ⚔ **RLVs:** Yes, if they are Sanguinarian vampires, but there are other types of RLVs.

- ⚔ **H&F:** Yes. Nearly all H&F vampires are depicted as being blood-feeders.

- ⚔ **RPGers:** Sometimes. They may incorporate blood fetishism into their role playing.

Do they kill those they feed from?

- ⚔ **RLVs:** No, unless they are criminals, or mentally unstable. A Sanguinarian almost always acquires blood from a willing donor, and does their best to never cause harm or severe injury to their donor.

⋏ **H&F:** Usually. Many older stories depict vampires as killers, while newer versions may show them as having more compassion, and allowing their victims to live.

⋏ **RPGers:** No, unless they are criminals, or mentally unstable.

Can they "turn" someone by feeding the person their blood?

⋏ **RLVs:** No. RLVs do not typically believe in the concept of "turning" or "sireing"

⋏ **H&F:** Sometimes. Most vampires are depicted as being able to make new vampires by feeding the person their blood. Some newer versions suggest that vampirism is a virus, or transmitted by other means.

⋏ **RPGers:** No. While they may claim they can, they cannot.

Do they sleep in coffins?

- ⅄ **RLVs:** Sometimes, but not often. It's a matter of personal preference.

- ⅄ **H&F:** Usually, though some stories only show a need for homeland earth, while others can rest wherever they choose.

- ⅄ **RPGers:** Sometimes, but not often. It's a matter of personal preference, and usually done only to enhance the roll.

Do they speak in Old English or other "dead" languages?

- ⅄ **RLVs:** Not usually, though they may well be able to speak more than one language, if they've taken the time to learn

- ⅄ **H&F:** Often, but not always. Eloquence is common among H&F vampires, but depending on the tale and time-frame, they may talk just like any average person.

- ⚔ **RPGers:** Often, if they believe it helps accentuate their character.

Do they have long nails and fangs?

- ⚔ **RLVs:** Sometimes, it's a matter of personal preference. Some RLVs have naturally long canines, some wear prosthetics, and some have their canines altered by a dentist.

- ⚔ **H&F:** Nearly all H&F vampires have fangs or sharp teeth, and may have long nails or claws.

- ⚔ **RPGers:** Sometimes, it's a matter of personal preference. Some RPGers have naturally long canines, some wear prosthetics, and some have their canines altered by a dentist.

Frequently Asked Questions About Vampires

Am I a Vampire? and other Frequently Asked Questions

Am I a Vampire? Are you a Vampire? Can you turn me into a vampire? These are questions that are commonly heard in the vampire community. They are questions that can be difficult, if not impossible to answer. I'll attempt to address them here to the best of my ability.

Questions about vampires

Q: Am I a Vampire?

A: I couldn't even begin to tell you. Some people say they can spot other vampires, but I think you are the only one who could truly know what you are or are not. What are the symptoms of being a vampire? There are plenty, and their validity varies depending on whom you ask. Sensitivity to sunlight, heightened sense of hearing/sight/smell, empathic/telepathic ability, pale skin, intense or abnormal eye color, pronounced canines, affinity for the night/darkness, nocturnal habits, interest in/taste for blood, being born with hair/teeth/birthmarks, being born on a holy day… all these and more have been considered signs of being a vampire. They can also be signs of a medical disorder of one sort or another.

Before you go thinking you're a Creature of the Night, go to a reputable physician and get yourself checked out. Rule out all reasonable medical explanations first. If you think you're hundreds of years old, immortal, Dracula, Lestat, Nosferatu, etc., you may want to seek a psychiatrist. Don't get me wrong, I'm not trying to be rude or condescending, but unless you can prove your claims beyond any shadow of doubt, you may have a mental disorder, and you should seek help. It's bad enough that many people who are vampires (or believe themselves to be) suffer from severe depression, isolation, and even suicidal tendencies. Yearning for blood or psychic energy, trying to find people who will accept and understand you, figuring out where you fit in, it can all take its toll on one's mental health. Being part of the Darkness is not glamorous, fun or status-enhancing. You will most likely be considered weird, or a freak, you will not have people flocking to your side, you won't get rich, and you may likely become very lonely and miserable.

Q: Can you make me into a Vampire?

A: No. And even if I could, I wouldn't. As stated above, it's not really a life you'd choose if you had any sense. I don't believe that anyone can be made into a vampire, "turned", "embraced", or whatever popular term you'd like to use. If you can prove it's possible, feel free. I think, more likely than not, if you are a Vampire, Kindred, Otherkin, or what-have-you, you were born that way. I've never met a beautiful immortal creature with the ability to drain one's blood, replace it with their own, and turn someone into a creature like themselves. There have been people who claim they can do just that, but I'd be wary, there are a lot of mentally unstable characters in this world who would prey on the innocence and naiveté of a sad, lonely person looking for acceptance and love.

You should also be wary of "Houses", "Clans" and the like. Not to say that there aren't wonderful groups out there that can help you on your path and give you safety and acceptance, there surely are, but there are also cults and dangerous individuals out there who would seek to use and hurt you.

Research any organization as fully as you can before entering. Talk to other members, and trust your gut. If something feels off, it probably is.

Q: Are Vampires real?

A: Yes, no, and I don't know. Confused? Join the club. Are there immortals that have lived for centuries feeding on the blood of unsuspecting humans? Not to my knowledge, but I haven't met everyone in the world, so I couldn't say for certain, but I doubt it. Are there mortal humans who feed on blood and live out a vampire-like lifestyle? Definitely. Real Living Vampires (RLV's), Sanguinarians, Psi-Vamps and others do exist. They are everywhere, and you may already know some of them, whether you're aware of it or not. They are typically average people, with homes, jobs, lovers, bills and all the stuff that everyone else has. They may have heightened abilities, vampiric habits and such, but they probably don't broadcast it publicly. Discretion is key in the vampire community. Are there vampires, werewolves, demons, etc.? Who knows? Anything is possible. I've never seen an atom, but I know they exist. I've never seen a God or Demon, but I believe they exist. The world is full of mysteries; you can never know what's out there.

Q: Are all vampires beautiful/Goth/insert other stereotypical description here?

A: Simply put, no. Humans who are vampires, live the vampire lifestyle, etc., are just as diverse as any other group of people. While it isn't uncommon for people in the vampire culture to dress in gothic attire, they don't all do it. It can depend on a lot of things, including, but not limited to: personal taste, whether they'll be in the general public or among friends and like-minded individuals, local climate and other factors. And don't assume that every Goth is a vampire, either. The way a person dresses doesn't automatically put them into any particular social group. As for looks, while I've seen some people in the vampire community that were positively stunning, I have seen ones that were just average, and some that were downright ugly. Appearance is a matter of genetics (or in some cases, of surgical manipulation). Basically, never judge a book by its cover. If you want to know what/who someone is, get to know them. Ask. There's no sure way to tell just by looking.

Q: Is there a Vampire religion?

A: I believe there is at least one, and probably more, group or groups that consider themselves to be a religion. In all honesty, I don't believe that vampirism is a religion; it is a way of life and who you are. I get that nasty hair-standing-up-on-my-neck feeling when I think of vampire religions, because, to me, it just screams CULT. I do know for a fact that you don't have to be part of a vampire religion to be a vampire, and in fact, many vampires have their own religious beliefs. I, myself, am Pagan, as are many other vamps that I know. There are also a lot of atheist vampires, and I have no doubt that there are Muslim, Christian, Catholic and other ones. Religion is a personal thing, and who or what you are does not mean you have to belong to any particular sect or belief system.

Q: I'm a vampire, so I don't have to worry about AIDS or STDs, right?

A: WRONG! Just because you're a vampire (or think you are) doesn't mean you're immune to disease or illness. Your body is still just as human as any other. Blood-born diseases and sexually transmitted diseases are a very real concern for every person on the planet. You are no exception. You can get sick, get a disease, and die just like anyone else. If you think otherwise, I feel very sorry for you and anyone who cares for you. Sexual activity and blood activities should never be taken lightly. You can catch disease, and also spread it to others. Always exercise care when doing anything that involves exchanging of bodily fluids, and always take care of yourself. Eat right, get plenty of rest, and stay active.

Q: As a vampire, will I be stronger/faster/smarter than others?

A: Nope. Being a vampire doesn't change you or your natural abilities. If you truly are a vampire, during your awakening you may realize abilities you didn't know you had, but believe me when I say that they were already there. You can also have "abnormal" abilities, and not be a vampire. If you want to be smarter, take a course in something, or read more. If you want to be stronger or faster, exercise or take up a sport. If you want to fly, become a pilot or take up skydiving. As far as other abilities, such as empathy, energy reading, etc., some people say they can be learned, but I think it's just a matter of finding the abilities that were already within you from birth. We all have our gifts, it's up to you to find yours.

Q: I'm a vampire, so I don't need to eat regular food anymore, right? I can just live on blood?

A: No. A human body cannot sustain life on blood alone. As a matter of fact, our bodies aren't even really designed to process blood for nutrition, and too much can make you very ill. RLVs eat food, and we rather enjoy it. Regardless of whether you're psi or sang, you still need food and water and all that good stuff. As a matter of fact, it's not uncommon for sangs to use certain foods as blood substitutes. At any rate, food and drink are necessities, just like sleep and air. Anyway, would you really want to live without chocolate?

Frequently Asked Questions About Me

Am I a Vampire? and other Frequently Asked Questions

Am I a Vampire? Are you a Vampire? Can you turn me into a vampire? These are questions that are commonly heard in the vampire community. They are questions that can be difficult, if not impossible to answer. I'll attempt to address them here to the best of my ability.

Questions about me

Q: Are you a Vampire?

A: Speaking for myself, it can be foolhardy, and even dangerous, to attach a label such as that to oneself.

Do you have what are commonly considered vampiric traits and tendencies? In short, yes. Does that in itself make me a vampire? Probably not.

Do you have an affinity for, or attraction to vampires and vampiric things? Well, YEAH. I run a vampire site, don't I?

Do you think you're immortal/will die in the sun/insert other ridiculous concept here? Of course not. I'm just as mortal as you or anyone else. If you think you're immortal, I'd love to see you prove it. (Said with extreme sarcasm) While I am rather sensitive to the sun, it won't kill me, unless, of course, I were to stay out in it for days on end without food or water. I love garlic and silver. I don't like crosses or crucifixes, but they won't make my skin light on fire if you hold one against me.

Would you die if I staked/beheaded you? Um, YEAH, those methods would kill ANYTHING.

Please try to take my sarcasm with a grain of salt; I've heard some pretty ridiculous claims and accusations in my day. And if you think I'm being evasive, I am. Even if I were a vampire, I wouldn't go blabbing it to the world, and neither should you. There are some seriously crazy people in this world, and God knows what you could get yourself into. Even admitting a mere interest in vampires can be dangerous in some circles.

I know that some may say that if you're not willing to stand up and shout that you're a vampire, then you're really not, but if you pay attention, you'll see that most RLVs are very private people. We do our part and speak our piece, but we don't go around waving red banners at the world.

Q: Why do you have a vampire site when there are already so many of them on the 'net?

A: Because I think it's important to have resources for real vampires (psi and sang) with different points of view and different information. As much as we may try, I don't think any one webmaster can cover all the topics, or get all the information that people will want and put it into one place. I'm doing my very best to make a site that is attractive, informational, and entertaining. I also want to be able to express my experiences and my point of view. No one person has all the right answers. Also, there are a lot of sites out there that frighten, misinform, or mislead the people that come to them. I want people to have a place they can come to that is accurate, up-to-date, and safe.

Q: What are you doing for the vampire community?

A: I'm trying to provide a resource for real vampires, entertainment and education for vampire fans, and a safe new place for RLVs to share their thoughts. I know my site hasn't been around that long, and I haven't had much of a chance to really get into the community, but all things come with time. I have plans for a lot of things. Even if I'm not writing a book or getting interviewed on TV, I can still do my part from here and try to make a difference in the community, and educate people outside it for the benefit of our collective safety and happiness.

Have We Been Misinformed About Vampires?

Have vampires intentionally given us bad intel?

Going on the hypothesis that vampires in the mythological sense actually exist, is it possible they they have misinformed us to keep people from hunting and killing them, and to allow them to exist in our society?

In an early episode of the popular HBO series True Blood, Bill Compton and Sookie Stackhouse have a conversation about the truth as it relates to vampires. Bill stated that humans were misinformed to protect vampires from danger. If vampires are really among us, do you think they've been misinforming us?

It actually makes a lot of sense if you think about it. Consider how much danger it can put a person in to admit that they're homosexual or transsexual. It's often safer to hide what you are, and lead people to believe something else, thereby allowing you to live some semblance of a normal life. It would make perfect sense for vampires to misdirect us to maintain their own safety.

Can you imagine what it would be like if there were easy ways to tell if someone was a vampire, or even test for it? Maybe they've lead us to believe that they react badly to silver and holy water so that if we splash someone or press silver to them and they have no reaction we'd think they must be human. Maybe they've created stories of vampires having no reflection so if we stick a mirror in their face we won't think they're the walking undead.

Many of the myths and legends surrounding vampires make little or no sense, and could easily have been made up by real vampires to throw people off. Being confined to darkness, having an aversion to garlic, being OCD about counting seeds and other such stories could have been the result of strange superstition or deliberate misinformation.

If you believe that mythological vampires exist, it would be very sensible for them to fill people's brains with all these ideas over the ages to protect the safety of their race. My earlier examples are good ones, as no real vampire would want people to know their actual weaknesses and telltale signs. After ages of reinforcement through literature and film, there are things people now accept as absolute truth about vampires.

Case in point, lots of vampire aficionados were up in arms over the movie Twilight. "Real Vampires Don't Sparkle" has become a catch-phrase, even adorning the fronts of t-shirts and bumper stickers. People were also upset with the Twilight vampires' ability to walk in the daylight. I have seen similar unhappy comments about the new ABC series The Gates, where a liberal slathering of sunscreen allows the area's vamps to enjoy daytime social activities. But we all know vamps are creatures of the night, right?

Perhaps we don't know nearly as much as we think we do about what vampires really are and what their weaknesses are. We all know that there are RLVs living among us (Real Living Vampires), but for all we know, the mythological vampires are out there too, walking among us, enjoying the centuries of misinformation they've fed us that allow them to exist alongside us completely unnoticed.

If You Were a Vampire, Who Would You Eat?

Bad guys are so tasty...

In movies, television and books we've seen some vampires make a conscious choice as to who or what they feed on. If you were a vampire, who would you feed on to survive?

Some vampires, depending on the mythology used, have the option of feeding on animals to stay alive, and in some stories we have seen them do just that. In an attempt to blend in with modern society or maintain more of their humanity, they will feed on animals for blood, rather than feeding on humans. However, there are many myths which state that a vampire can only survive on human blood. In these cases, a vampire might face some moral or ethical questions when it comes to feeding, which they must do in order to survive.

For the sake of this article, we're going to eliminate the vampire stories in which our blood-sucking night stalkers can acquire and feed on bagged blood from a hospital, and there is no such thing as simulated blood. We're going to talk about vampires who can only survive on the blood of a living human being, and nothing else will suffice. We're also going to assume that willing victims are few and far between.

I have seen some vampires simply give in to their beastly nature and feed on whatever unwary human happens to pass by. These vampires tend to be violent and evil, and we are meant not to like them because they show no control, and no respect for other forms of life. Other vampires make choices about what type of people they feed on, based on their own personal ethics and morals. As viewers we like these vampires more, because they are showing some restraint, and they are being conscientious as to who they feed on and why.

So what criteria do these kinds of vampires use to choose their prey? Well, some kill those who do evil. By feeding on murderers, rapists, abusers, swindlers and other doers of evil acts, they feel that they're doing a service to the world. Every meal is one less hardcore criminal on the streets. Others feed on the homeless or junkies. Again, these vampires feel that they're providing a community service because they're cleaning up the scum of the earth. Still others will feed on the diseased (for vampires that are totally immune to human diseases) as a service to prevent these people from spreading their illnesses to others. Some even feed on the wealthy, as many of them tend to be less than scrupulous individuals.

So, if you were a vampire, who would you feed on? Would you eat rich people, evil people, the homeless, the diseased, or just anyone who happened by? Would you kill everyone you fed from, or would you try to leave them alive? If you left them alive, would you feed on the same people over and over again, or would you never hit the same victim twice? I think it's an interesting set of questions, and it might say something about the kind of person you are.

I think if I were a vampire I'd probably feed on whoever was convenient at the time, and I'd do my best never to kill or seriously maim anyone. However, I would be on the lookout for heinous criminals. If I knew the guy on the street corner was a pedophile or a murderer, I'd feed from him and kill him. Now, I know many might disagree with the idea of vigilante justice, but hey, why not save the cops some time and money? I'd be making the world a safer place and getting a meal at the same time. Sounds like a pretty sweet deal to me.

Paid to Donate Blood for Vampires

Would you donate to a vamp?

If vampires came out of the coffin, would you become a blood donor to help keep peace between the human race and vampires? What if they offered to pay you?

True Blood and other movies and stories have presented the idea of vampires becoming public knowledge. In True Blood, vampires came out because of synthetic blood. Since we don't have that kind of technology yet, a scenario like Daybreakers might be more likely, where vampire feeding habits dwindle the human population. However, if vampires came out, there might be a solution.

I've read some vampire stories that introduced the idea of humans being paid to donate blood to vampires. Honestly, there's a part of the goth/vamp subculture that currently exists who would gladly donate to a real vampire, but there are not enough of them to satisfy the hunger of an entire race. To avoid the decimation of the human race, paid donors could become popular.

The idea is much like that of normal blood donation, only instead of donating to the Red Cross, you donate to an individual vampire or vampire family. Whether blood is taken through biting or more professional extraction would be a personal decision between donor and vampire. In return for providing this life-sustaining fluid, you would be compensated.

Perhaps you might just get a pay check, whatever the vampire in question thinks is reasonable based on the frequency of donation. In some cases, with regular donation, you may become more like a pampered pet, having all your needs provided for to keep you healthy and happy and providing blood for a long time to come.

Some people might find the idea offensive, while others would readily accept it. For those less fortunate, providing blood in exchange for a home and protection might be a deal too good to resist. It really wouldn't be much different from twenty-something men and women who exchange sex for money and gifts, it would be similar to having a sugar daddy/mamma, only sex wouldn't need to be part of the equation. (Although for some, it might be appealing.)

If the world took that turn, would you become a donor? I know I would. It would behoove a vampire to keep their donor healthy, happy and safe. If someone were to offer me a home, food and the things I desire (as well as protection from harm) in exchange for my blood, I'd be more than happy. Not only would it benefit me, it would keep at least one vampire from feeding on an unwilling victim, thereby making the world a little bit safer.

That last point is what people might want to consider in the event this hypothetical situation were ever to become reality. If vampires are any kind of rational being, they would likely prefer willing donors over random victims. It would keep the food supply alive, and keep them from being hunted as ravenous monsters. If people were willing to become donors, they would be protecting themselves and others as well.

We may never know if there are vampires among us, but it doesn't hurt to think ahead and plan for the possibility. If vampires are real, and they have been able to live among us without notice all this time, it's likely they would be willing to negotiate with their food source to keep a peaceful world.

The Vampire Satanist Connection

Why people seem to think vampires and Satanists are the same thing

I've learned over the years that many, if not most people think that anyone in the vampire community is a Satanist. While some of them are, most of them aren't. It's an ugly stereotype perpetuated by uneducated people.

Much the way people often lump Pagans and Satanists in the same category, Vampires and Satanists are being lumped together as well. They are in no way the same thing, and being one does not automatically make you the other, but uneducated people with religious bias keep spreading this ugly misconception.

In a way, I understand why people think all vampires are Satanists. People perceive vampires as evil, and if one is engaging in and professing to be something evil, then they must be worshiping Satan. (Interesting side note; most Satanists don't actually worship Satan, they believe in self over any deity.) The thing is, Real Living Vampires are no more evil than any other person. They are human, and they are capable of the same greatness and atrocities as any other human.

The truth is, there *are* vampires who are Satanists, but there are also vampires who are Pagan, Christian, Catholic, Buddhist and a slew of other religions. They're *people*, and people believe in a variety of things. It's been my experience that very few RLVs are Satanists. I've found more of them to be Pagan, Spiritualist or Atheist than anything else. Many real life vampires, being something outside of the norm, do explore various religions, and may convert to a different path than that of their families and friends. However, their choices are as widely varied as that of any other subculture group.

Another reason for people assuming that vampires are Satanists stems from the fact that many young people come to a rebellious stage in life, and things like vampirism and Satanism become temporarily alluring. The thing is, these kids are lost and striking out against parents and society, and most of the time they know nothing about the lifestyles they're playing at. Their spiteful and violent activities done under the guise of being a vampire or Satan worshiper simply make real vampires and Satanists look bad.

Cults are another reason for the stereotype. Cults often use things that will be appealing to lost, scared teens and other people. Vampires and the power of Satan seem wonderful in comparison to their miserable mundane lives. Unfortunately, we hear more in the media about Satanic and Vampire cults than we do about the real thing, and it makes everyone look bad. The sad truth is that these cults are just using a part of reality in a twisted way to lure the vulnerable into their trap.

People should really do their research when it comes to both Vampires and Satanists. I have been involved with people of both types, and they were some of the best people I've ever encountered. If you didn't ask what they were, you'd never know that they were any different from anyone else. You could very well work with or live next to a real vampire or Satanist, and you'd never have a clue.

Vampire Cults Give Sanguinarians a Bad Name

Vampire cults make life difficult for Real Living Vampires

Real Living Vampires and Sanguinarians are not the demons they're sometimes made out to be. Cults and rebellious teenagers make vampire society look bad, but there's little truth to the stories you may have heard.

Vampire cults have been popping up all over, and have probably become even more widespread with the recent popularity of vampires in movies and books. These people make it difficult for real vampires, who have nothing in common with those dangerous individuals. If you do just a little research though, you'll find that Sanguinarians and other vampires are not really something to fear.

Vampire Cults tend to employ a combination of mythical allure, brainwashing, pseudo-Satanism and other tactics to lure unfortunate individuals. I have heard of these groups having orgies, public blood-lettings, slavery, human and animal sacrifice and all sorts of horrid behavior. Most real vampires would find all of this appalling.

Real Living Vampires are not monsters out to control the minds of local youth. They're regular people who happen to have a need for blood or energy. Sanguinarian vampires tend to be the most maligned because they feed on blood. While feeding on blood (usually human blood) is a part of a Sang's life, they don't take it by force, and the idea of sacrifices would turn the stomach of most. Life is sacred to a real vampire, and not something to be wasted for the sake of ritual.

Society believes that sex, vampires and Satan go hand-in-hand, and that adds to the allure of cults, and the bad reputation of Sangs and other vampires. Sanguinarians probably don't have any more sex than anyone else. Some vampires, Psychic Vampires in particular, can derive energy from sexual acts, but they're not out having orgies to get it. It's also a horrid myth that all vampires are Satanists. Vampires come in as many faiths as any other subculture.

It's a sad fact that extremist groups of any kind can give the whole group a bad name. It happens in many faiths and subcultures that the horrible acts of the few cloud the truth about the many. Sanguinarians and Real Vampires in general are just like anyone else. They're human, they have jobs, they love, hate, and experience life pretty much like everyone else. If you met a real vampire tomorrow, you'd probably never even know it. Try not to let those who do wrong color your opinion of an entire portion of society.

Inexpensive Goth and Vamp Decorating

Find great Gothic and Vampire style décor for less

For those of us who enjoy Goth and Vamp style, it can be hard to decorate without spending a fortune on special items. I'll give you some tips for getting vampire and goth decorations at inexpensive prices.

When you're looking to do any kind of home decorating on a budget, you need to get creative. Thinking outside the box can be your biggest asset in finding or making great decorations. When you're doing Gothic, Victorian or vampire style decorating, you need to get especially creative.

When you're out and about, look for scarves and bandanas. These can be used as table covers, curtain tie-backs, they can be wrapped around lamps, hung on walls flat or in a swag or wrapped around bedposts. You can also look in the fabric section of your superstore or craft store for remnants. These are what's left after most of a bolt of fabric has been sold. You can sometimes find really great fabric for decorating.

Find doilies and lace tablecloths on clearance or at yard sales and flea markets. The older they look, the better it is. You can dye these items any color to fit your room's theme. Another great trick for making doilies and tablecloths look antique is to soak them in coffee or tea to give them an authentic aged look. This can also be done with other fabrics. You can also splatter thinned red paint or red wine on fabric for the illusion of blood stains. If you have some red beat, you could opt to use the real thing, but I strongly suggest a good wash afterward.

Fabric stores often carry a wide variety of lace and tassels that can be used to decorate with. You can hang tassels from light chains and lamp pulls, or add them to curtain tie-backs. Lace can be used for tie-backs, wrapped around bed frames or the body of a lamp, sewn onto the edges of pillowcases and napkins or tied around vases or bouquets of fake flowers. If you know someone creative, you can even have lace crocheted for you in the color of your choice.

Check the bargain bin and clearance area of your craft and superstores for fake flowers. I have found flowers in dark colors like blue, black and purple in these bins. Dark colors don't sell as well as brighter and lighter colors, so they often go on clearance. You can use fake flowers in a variety of ways for decorating, not just in vases. If the flowers aren't coated, you can dye white or light flowers in diluted acrylic paint or food coloring. You can also use spray paint to change the color of some silk flowers.

It can be difficult to find strings of lights in colors that appeal to the darker set, but there's a way around that. If you can get strings of standard holiday lights, you can pull out all the bulbs and put them back to create strings of the colors you prefer. It takes a lot of time, but sometimes it's the only way. If you're lucky, you can snag light strings of odd colors during the holidays.

Of course, one of the easiest way to get Goth and vampire decorating items on the cheap is to shop your dollar stores and superstores during and after

Halloween. This is the time when the widest variety of dark and unusual items are available. If you shop after Halloween, you can catch a lot of items on sale at enormous discounts. And don't overlook costumes! You can dismantle costumes for the fabric and other parts, and convert them into decorations.

If you want to get more ideas on ways to turn inexpensive items into home decorations, I recommend looking up Halloween crafts online. You can begin to get ideas of how to turn common materials into unique items. With a little creativity, you can start snagging all sorts of inexpensive items and turning them into your very own Gothic and Vampire home decorations.

In Closing

Final Words

I hope this book has opened your eyes in regards to vampires, both real and mythical. I enjoyed writing it, and I will likely write quite a bit more in the future, so keep your eyes open for a second volume.

Best Wishes!

Briana Blair

www.ingramcontent.com/pod-product-compliance
Lightning Source LLC
Chambersburg PA
CBHW072204280526
45788CB00002B/874